The Ground Never Lets Go

The Ground Never Lets Go
poems

---

by Liz Marlow

~ 2026 ~

The Ground Never Lets Go

Editor-in-chief
Eric Morago

Operations Associate
Shelly Holder

Associate Editors
Mackensi E. Green
Allysa Murray
Rob Sturma
Ellen Webre

Editor Emeritus
Michael Miller

Cover art
Fear by Felix Nussbaum

Cover design
Eric Morago

Book design
Michael Wada

Moon Tide logo design
Abraham Gomez

The Ground Never Lets Go
is published by Moon Tide Press

Moon Tide Press
6709 Washington Ave. #9297
Whittier, CA 90608
www.moontidepress.com

FIRST EDITION

Printed in the United States of America

ISBN # 978-1-957799-99-5

Contents

G-d

Even as a child, I knew to leave
out the o—its nod to moons,
planets, stars, and spiral galaxies.

All things down to their microscopic
makeup are round—atoms
and their structure. Yahwists,

egocentrics believing His focus
was an ideal Vitruvian Man,
could not have imagined other planets

while writing Genesis, so when I leave
out the o, I leave science behind.
When I write the dash—a closed eye

in prayer—I apply tradition. If I were
to trade the dash for an o, I would
become a gravedigger—covering

paper with a pall like the shrouds
my grandparents and their parents
wore. I will wear one

after the Chevra Kadisha—
group of Jews trained to purify—
writes dashes across my body

with wet sponges, preparing me
for death as a nurse in the hospital
prepared me for life. After I have

settled into the dash-shaped
simple pine box, without nails, without
metal hinges, to become one with earth

and all its organisms as my ancestors
went and descendants will go, I will
break down into ordinary atomic matter.

I.

Freedom to dig the common earth, to drink
the universal air—for this they sought…

— Emma Lazarus, "In Exile"

Esther's Curfew

Venetian Ghetto, March 1516

Moses raised almond wood and water
walls, dried a path—
    gate open
        for refugees
        (abused immigrants),
    gate closed
        on oppressors
        (guards, soldiers, police).

A bell creates a labyrinth
of canals,
(the beginning).
    First day—
        awaken.
    Second day—
        listen,
        look up
        to sky masked
        with stones, ceilings.

A wall is a corset.
    Third day—
        dike separating
        flood and drought.

A bell rings
(the end).
    Fourth day—
        summoning mass, labor.
        Doors close
        on us.

The sun is a yellow hat.
A star is a patch
of light.
    Fifth day—
        livestock penned.
    Sixth day—
        prisoner.

There is no rest.

Rivka Survives

Skvira, Ukraine Pogrom, 1919

Purple swirls on my breasts, belly—crystal balls—reveal my fate. Not all that grows is made from love—when a bee pollinates a sunflower, it is to take the nectar. He handled my skin like an aphid on a leaf while I clawed at him like a dormouse burrowing for the winter. Someone, a sister, might have asked, *What was your first time like?* Hands ungloved during snowfall, scabs peeled away, what should remain concealed was exposed. A face should be bare, but he veiled mine—pulling up my skirt. Were his eyes the color of dead grass? Was his mouth jagged, a cemetery full of crumbling tombstones? His breath smelled of vodka. Mine smelled of garlic. His words—a dull knife. My words—crouching in an empty well. His skin was of metal. Mine was of dust. What does the past look like when time is a shovel? What does night look like without the sky? How do I flee without a map? Earth is of a magnetic field. The ocean is of an undertow.

Sara's Mother Teaches Her How to Prepare Onion Soup

Beef, bones, and root vegetables bubble
in water. Once the stock thickens,
Mama shows me how to avoid tears
while peeling and chopping
an onion. *Get it cold. Let snow fall on it.*
Her blade divides the sweet,
savory snowball. No saltiness.
Usually, her knife quickens on the cutting
board, but she slows for me, revealing
how clawing the onion and letting the blade
slide up and down—never fully lifting it
from the wood—protects skin from the slice.
Butter sizzles in the pan, ready to caramelize.
Onion pieces fall from her fingers like snow
held tight to branches too long.
Wine adds a layer of flavor. Croutons
add texture. Papa tells me how they once
tasted this soup from porcelain
on white tablecloths as candlelit halos
rested on her shoulders, that she
immediately recognized its exact recipe,
the way a painter looks at the sunset
and knows which colors and brushstrokes
to use on a canvas. I imagine painting
her tearless face—capturing steam
that glistens her skin and fills
the room with warmth, capturing
this moment of her teaching me
how to make it without her.

Sara Visits Avraham's Tailor Shop

Berlin, 1933

Fabric bolts line the walls of Papa's shop—
solid linen resembling shades of sand,
pinstripes so thin they seem to disappear,
and plaids mapping coordinates of touch.
I imagine Papa spooling silk, weaving it
on a loom. Does he imagine me, Mama,
and his customer as mulberry larvae
to protect, cover with silk strands?
After pinning cuffs on pants and a jacket,
avoiding skin, protecting cloth from blood,
he asks me if I've washed my hands. After
examining them for dirt camouflaged
by freckles, he says, *Feel the fabrics
in your hands,* and I imagine meters
of silk the hue of oceanwater—a wave
rolling on my skin—or becoming
a queen covered from neck to ankles
in gold embroidered red velvet
with pearl and glass beads. When we
get home, I draw a picture of my crown,
turn Papa's umbrella into my scepter,
and Mama's full crystal candy dish
becomes my glittering sovereign's orb—
its globe shape symbolizing G-d's
power with each piece of candy,
a jewel from a conquered land.

Sara's First Lesson with Her New Piano Teacher

Berlin, 1937

She, who guards all the keys,
believes that my fingers do not
belong on them. Nonetheless,
she says, *Curve your fingers*
like your nose. Let them drift off
the keyboard during a rest, the way
your Jew hair floats off your shoulders
in the breeze. Their ivory feels smooth
like eggshells on my fingertips, and I
treat them delicately as such—keys
glossy like the albumen after I tap
my spoon to crack open a hard
boiled egg and tear it apart as it
sits in its cup—upright in perfect
posture. Her curio cabinet is full
of porcelain eggcups, one for each
day of the month with different
flowery details. I imagine her
thinking, *I will devour what was once*
nestled under a hen—protected—
using this blue rose cup or maybe this
one with daffodils, while I imagine
myself becoming something harder—
a petrified dinosaur egg or not
even an egg at all—the piano lid,
not properly propped open,
ready to slam shut.

Consul General Feng-Shan Ho and Rabbi Shimon Sholom Kalish Discuss the Jewish Question

Both men bow
like bars of jail
doors bending
from blowtorches.
One bows habitually,
both respectfully.
The younger,
a plum blossom
not understanding
a trumpet pitcher plant's desire
to devour a butterfly,
asks why the rabbi's people are hated.
The rabbi combs his fingers
through his beard,
the way he might have
once raked a garden
before planting seeds.
Because we have hair
dark like river mud,
skin the color of sand.
Somewhere,
a hippo is saving a baby
zebra from drowning
as it crosses a river
during migration.
Somewhere else,
a dolphin is coaxing
a beached whale
back into the ocean.
After traveling down
rivers and across seas,
like an Arctic tern searching
for a place to live,
entire families will move
far from home.

German Jews Travel from Genoa, Italy to Shanghai, China via the SS Victoria Cruise Liner

August 1937

Last week, some of us
held children with swelled
bellies, starving. Here,
we swell from truffle sauce,
pecorino, filet mignon,
and desserts—endless.
Yesterday, we passed
a bloated whale carcass. Sharks
tore away skin to reveal red
the way the young
tear away lovers' clothes.
Now, life here is wide-eyed.
Flowers in ceramic pots blink
open their petals in wonder
of how we ended up here
as waiters water them
from silver pitchers.
Then there are memories of life—
mahogany bannisters,
pillows filled with goose feathers,
the piano in the ballroom
with ivory keys,
tallow soaps at sinks.

Avraham's Tailor Shop

Kristallnacht, November 9-10, 1938

Waists puff out; legs, backs straighten
for the measuring.
A needle has
the power

to stitch together what tore, what was
always separated or reveal blood.
Shards tear skin into red
ribbons. A single boot
turns breath into
a zephyr.

Their sea of hammers reveals sidewalks
blanketed with splintered doors,
shattered windows—
a mosaic.

What image should I create
with my broom, dustpan?
A deity who sweeps
away righteous
instead of
wicked?

At what point in looking back, will
one of us become a pillar of salt?
They smash it all in His name
or against His name,
but what they rip,
we cannot
always
darn.

Sara Spins Her Dreidel the Night Before Her Father, Avraham, Leaves to Find Work

Chanukah, 1939

נ *(Nun)*
Afraid of the icy ground, dying
leaves, needles, petals cling
to their homes. New moon. There is no
such thing as nothing.

ג *(Gimel)*
My family tree is a full
menorah on the last night.
Mama, shammash, lights the others
while our flames spin, dance.

ה *(Hay)*
I peal foil off coins
not used for currency—
gelt. A thin piece of chocolate
cannot fill a stomach.

Nearby, caterpillars hanging
only halfway in this world
hibernate under leaf litter
ready to awaken as moths, butterflies.

ש *(Shin)*
Ante up to play this game, all games.
Hunger growls. Storms steal seeds,
throw them into fresh soil.
There, saplings take root.

Avraham Leaves His Family Behind to Find Work

Prague, December 1939

Real men do not wear stars.
They say. Real men get paid
for rock-hard skin on hands,

storm breath, sun-soaked collars.
Real men drink
ripples—crisp down the throat,

sleep in beds ready to spread
wings. Up a side street, a man turns
breath into a red glass ball ornament,

invites me inside
for a burning shot
of herb and spice liqueur,

offers me a job. My wife's face
emerges in a cloud
of dust, in clear glass,

or is that my distorted reflection?
At night, through the dim lights
of the Christmas market,

every girl resembles my daughter.
Her apparition rises
from a hot cup of mulled wine,

from a bag of roasted chestnuts.
She becomes a marionette
hanging from the edge

of a kiosk's roof in a breeze—
shivering, dancing to stay warm
while her eyes search for me.

Chaja Kubrzanska's Bath

Jedwabne, Poland Pogrom, June 25, 1941

For days after delivery,
my body, hollow bleeding,
hungered for a return of what
once was but also stood ready
to surrender what would become.
Ready for summer, what hibernates
is now out in the open, the way
my baby ascends from under
my shirt after nursing. A turtle
sunbathes on a half-submerged
log in this pond while a few
aquatic warblers click and sing
in the tall grass nearby until
an approaching accordion drowns
the song, scaring them away.
If I pray enough, maybe
they'll return to bathe with us.
If I pray enough, maybe
instruments will no longer
smother bellows,
eventually ceasing,
because men's arms tire
of swinging. Men,
wearing others' blood
on their faces like redcurrant
berries dotting the ground,
come here seeking more. Red
never ends. It reappears
year after year. And men,
they crave others' blood,
because butchers
steal the slaughter.
If I pray enough, maybe G-d
will let them bleed with us.

If I pray enough,
maybe they will drown in this
makeshift mikveh after
my baby and I face the water.

Matya's Separation

Szczuczyn, Poland Pogrom, June 28, 1941

In the expanse of deep breaths, Father snores,
and Mother cocoons herself back to infancy
as metal sharpens on stone. Should what
a man uses to slay a tree bear that name
when used to split our families into
many parts? If I hear cries last,
will G-d also greet me with
His? When our weeping
ends, will He stand
trial with us all?

Shmuel's Loss

Wąsosz, Poland Pogrom, July 5, 1941

Chipmunks transport
food in cheeks
stuffed like sacks
from the understory
through tunnels
to a bunker, priming
for winter, the way
Dad fills a silo
with grain, the way
Mom sews coats
from pelts of rabbits
I catch throughout
the year. Young
chipmunks devote
months to collecting
acorns dropped
from trees, while adults
spend mere days seeking
out the forest's heedless
immigrants with new
homes to plunder,
the way our neighbors
seek out shy refugees
fleeing shrapnel
and shards to come here,
a place stained
with iron, rot, silence.
If caught in the act,
a seasoned adult will
kill for what a young
family spent all fall
collecting. The labor
required for stockpiling

is too difficult,
but a fight, a fight
quickly decides
who will survive.

Rabbi Avigdor Białostocki's Dance

Jedwabne, Poland Pogrom, July 10, 1941

I.
Knives, sticks, stones. Wielders prod,
throw until their arms weaken. With
hammers, we break Lenin apart.
He was never ours, but here we are,
carrying him, mangled on a stretcher.

II.
While they shove sticks under our feet—
forcing dance—the ground might reimagine
itself waxed wood. Let me be clear. When
I bend my knees, it is for prayer, never a plié.

III.
Barns age like hair from brown to gray. Gray
holds tight to difference, revels in its shade.
Once the dolls ignite—some filled with straw,
others filled with life, turning back ends.
A barn can never be a barn again.

II.

Ten immutable rules, a moon
For mutable lampless men.

— Isaac Rosenberg, “The Jew”

Sara's Letter to Her Grandparents, Berlin

Dear Oma and Opa,

Bombs hit the zoo yesterday. This morning, I found a bright red feather on the sidewalk like an arrow of blood undecided where to lead me. It reminded me of the poppies we planted in your garden last year. Next time, do you think toucans and macaws from the aviary will know to fly away from bombs shaped like tree trunks? Will they know how to build new nests? They were so accustomed to living in cages.

Mama said the gunfire we heard was from keepers killing bears and tigers they raised as cubs, not trusting them to wander the streets. When it got loud, I burrowed myself under the bed. Mama hid in our empty pantry.

Are there poppies and tulips in the garden of your new house? You were supposed to write as soon as you got there, but we haven't heard from you. Let us know how you're getting settled.

Love,

Sara

Franz Stangl's White Clothes

They are all mine—
        mouths
        full of precious opals
        (some grayed from time).

Patching potholes,
crowning decay,
curing an ache,

their gold setting
        becomes a necklace
        or ring
        for my wife

as the goldsmith
(one of them)
grasps the only fire I want—
        power
        to raze if not wielded
        like an eraser
        to a single name
        scribbled in pencil
        on a list.

He melts
what is useful.
Everything else he touches
reveals what they are—
        soot,
        filth.

With their blood on his hands,
he pulls
gravestone teeth
like yanking hooks
from the mouths
of caught fish.

There is no use for gold
on dead animals.
Now it is mine.

They are all mine.

Mikhail's Soup

Tuchinka Pogrom, Minsk Ghetto, November 20, 1941

Mommy squeezes my hand like a balloon
string as we walk down the dead-end street.
She forgets, but I remind her of my soup
cooling and tummy grumbling while dogs
growl at our hands. Do we smell differently?
Mommy and I leave behind planets—
balls of bread spiraling in broth—
and my spoon bathing in my metal bowl.
Even before we opened the door, steam's fingers
seemed to direct us away from the house.
Now, she clutches her favorite red
leather handbag, and I carry my quilt.
It comforts her to think she needs money
where we're going, while I need warmth.

Avraham's New Home

Minsk Ghetto, November 20, 1941

Wooden doors greet me,
opening with oiled silence, but no blankets
or blue linens like clean water wait
to warm bodies. No feather pillows wait

to cradle cheeks. The ersatz floor
(without wooden planks, without
ceramic tiles) is an ersatz bed—
an imprint (crater) in the earth where

someone else rested, where I rest.
Rising steam invites me to eat ersatz
matzo ball soup—small chunks
of bread floating in a bowl of hot water—

at a wobbly table. On top of an old suitcase,
someone left an empty envelope,
an unfolded letter—ink still wet. One
of the letter's upturned corners rustles

like a hand gesturing for me to come closer,
ready to reveal it all if I choose to look—
while light, nearly blinding, shines through
the broken window's jagged glass teeth.

Mikhail's Letter, Minsk Ghetto

Dear Brother,

I wish I knew why you and Daddy left. Sometimes, Mommy holds your sweaters to her face like the bouquets of lilies Daddy gave her on holidays. Remember the honey spice cookies she baked on our birthdays? I imagine those cookies as I eat bread. Mommy says no one has sugar or honey anymore. Sometimes, I don't save some of my food for later, and my stomach will hurt from eating so much all at once. It's a much better feeling than hunger, though. Sometimes, Mommy yells at me for eating too much too quickly, but I don't let her see my tears. You told me never to let anyone see me cry, to be like *them*—firm, head held high.

Miss you,

Mikhail
20. November 1941

Avraham and the Fence

Minsk Ghetto, 1941

Behind barbed wire: fire
        flies, glowworms reveal
                their true nature in darkness.
Behind barbed wire: city
        lights compete with a sunrise.
                Out there, the forest's fog
becomes so dense, no one sees
        hands extend, no one
                notices shadows leading
until they touch, devour all.
        Out there, voices
                on radios never lie.
Here, a father tells a mother
        to leave the baby outside
                the door; older children
stay silent. *No one kills*
        babies. She will be safe.
                Out there, gunfire softens
in the rain. A mother
        crawls out of a mass grave
                and walks back here, shedding
earth with each step. She says,
        she forgot to put her children
                in her coat pocket,
kisses their faces in photos,
        says, she will never leave
                without them again.

Sara's Migration

When we arrive, Oma and Opa
will wave from the platform
as our train approaches the station.

Opa will twirl me like a falling
maple seed. Oma will pinch
my cheeks to test their ripeness.

Papa will smoke a brisket
to celebrate our new home. Mama
will make my favorite—borscht.

Memories fill my suitcase—Oma
singing *Shema* while we squinted
to find the faintest star and drawing

pilots or feathers on paper airplanes
with Opa. Our voices mimicked
engines and birdsong—my hum,

Opa's deep raven croak.
In one photo, I was old enough
to walk but craved Opa's arms.

As he held me, his shoulders
hunched, the way ours do now
from overstuffed suitcases.

Sara and the End

Majdanek, 1942

When the copper butterfly first
        emerged from the chrysalis—
                spread cape thin as silk
rising on the end of a runway—
        she felt a weight lift—
                cut hair, breeze on skin.
After hiding
        under leaf litter and dangling—
                shelled like a hazelnut—
all light blinded her,
        so she inhaled shadows,
                wrapped herself in her cape
bore rain and wind—
        stood still—
                waiting for the storm to pass.

Sara's Uniform

Majdanek, 1942

I wear these stripes—
streaks of tears through dirt,

a river's channels barren
where water once pushed

aside what stood in its way.
I wear shoes of bricks

pulled from a mausoleum.
As I lift a foot, which

descendant reveals their face—
imprint in gravel—what

could have been? I wear a halo
of smoke—sack

floating, hot air
balloon—on the platform,

hoping to land somewhere
I will see familiar faces.

Sara Contemplates Where Her Parents Might Be

Terezin, 1942

Papa
When he left us,
he might have slept
on velvet
warm with sighs,
or in a valley covered
with snow that never melts—
where a train ends.

Mama
When she left me,
I no longer cupped
my ear for children's
laughter in the distance
or listened for the kingfisher's song—
a warning
of approaching boots.

Without my parents—
in every crowd,
I am alone.

In a dream, I am a bolt
of fabric
patched from all
of Mama's head scarves—
some silk,
some wool.

In a different dream—
Papa reminds me
to unspool,
unravel;
Mama reminds me to sew.

Sara's Bed

Terezin, 1942

Dress / shroud—snow covering a mountain. It takes millennia for mountains to lose their peaks. Here, within weeks, women's breasts shrivel into uncertainty of whether milk will ever return. A woman / arroyo sleeps beside me, grieving the flash flood of monthly blood she says stopped coming months ago. She once said *they* see us as empty buckets—under patched roofs—left empty, without purpose, waiting. On the bunkbed—cage / coffin—this woman's shoulders, feet, hips push against mine in the night—our bodies / (עצי חיים) trees of life. Our bodies / shut eyelids as her breath expires.

Sara Imagines Herself a Golem

Terezin, 1942

I dip my finger into a puddle,
rippling the only mirror here.
If I were brave enough to look
at my face, draw what I see
on a sheet of paper, muddy
fingertips would smear away
truth (אמת) from my forehead,
leaving death (מת) behind, eyes
would be made of scars. Life
runs down my thighs—rivulets
shaped like long talons reddening
soil. If Mama saw me standing
in this puddle of myself, would
she become a willow, myrtle,
or palm tree where her leaves
would shade, protect, save
me? Someone else's mother
whispers of my blood, gives me
thin rags to soak up what I am—
scarred, shapeless. I tilt my head,
listening for my creator, but my
ears are made of chains, packed
with dirt. Everything here is filled
with dry earth, awaiting moisture
to make it malleable, to give it life.

Franz Stangl's Treblinka

Thousands of stacked fallen trees,
decimated by a storm, rest,
ready for bugs and mice
to make a kitchen out of them,
but this forest, missing crisp white
birch trees, rotting its own
blackening logs into carrion
flowers attracting flies,
needs a good, controlled burn. I order
someone else to strip away the leaves.
I order someone else to carve
into bark, leaving sap in streaks
like cubist paintings. I order someone
else to light the fire. Because I do not
blacken my white clothes and hands,
He releases me from guilt—
allowing it to diminish
from Sisyphus's rock to a fleck
of ash on one of my boots.

Sara and the Fox

Treblinka, November 1942

I remember looking into a frozen
pond, seeing my future
crack—in the distance,
a nebula consumed a house.
Kindling and logs popped stars
in fog. In the corner
of my eye, a fox faced
north, listened for prey, dove
into the snow, then clenched

a squealing mouse in his jaws.
He faces north. I am the mouse
he hunts. His
paws—coarse like a brick
wall, like lava after it cools,
like bones left in
ashes—grab at me. At once,
he creates and smolders
my fire, so I spit cinders
rather than the word, *No.*
If I could pick myself up,
piece together a full book
of matches, I would become
an inferno. I would burn
it all down. Watch me.

Sara's Hunger

Treblinka, 1942

Your desert mouth discovers
it can still salivate
as the kapo devours
a peppered, roasted

beet in front of you.
You imagine becoming his
starling's song
while all sound, words

become *beet* to you.
His eyes—not yet bruised
with hunger—look
into yours. With fat fingers

grabbing your wings, he
crushes your gray
plumage against the walls
of the latrine—hollow

bones nearly shattering as he
pushes himself into you,
engulfs you in waste.
You breathe,

dreaming of perfume—
jasmine filled *Joy*,
vanilla filled *Tabu*.
When his panting

stops, he pulls out
a raw beet from his
coat pocket, tosses
it to you. Hands fill

with the dry dirt
        it sheds. With eyes closed,
your mouth reddens
        with vinegar, onions, that beet

scrubbed, chopped, thrown
        into borscht—dill sprinkled,
topped with cream. You lick
        your dry lips, take a grainy bite.

The Infanticide of Puah

Papa used to take me fishing on the river. We'd mix soap and water to pour onto the bank, to cleanse the dirt of its dirtiness, to cleanse the earth of its worms while small, round cellophane pillows tried to suffocate them. As I scooped their wet bodies up, they wiggled away from my hands, away from the hook, toward their home. Then the poke, slice, a coiling body clenched itself around metal tearing into it. A plop in the water. Trout attracted to the struggle bit and swallowed before the water became all-consuming.

I first felt Puah as a poke with her finger—constant, unwavering. A weathervane pointing west. A dulled bayonet. Then she became a fist of resistance during the push. Eyes barely open. Eyes the color of ashes. In my dreams, Puah is a trout before the hook. In my dreams, she is a worm before the soap. No gurgle in the water. No gasp for breath.

III.

Not always as you see us now,
Have we been used to weep and sigh…

—Morris Rosenfeld, “Chanukah Thoughts”

Avraham Recalls His First Rosh Hashanah as a Married Man

Sobibor, September 1942

She was newness, apples—
her shofar voice summoned me home.

Body of honey, she rose, left
a constellation on the bed,

billowing lace curtains from
an open window—pregnant belly.

Now, wind whispers through feathers,
grass blades. By the time the branches

feel it, the sky has burst
at its seams, thrown all apples—

the hardened ground
rotting, ready to atone

for what it borrowed,
took without asking first.

Irena Sendler Saves Ava

Ava sips apple juice—
fizzy with barbiturates—
to hibernate
like a hedgehog
and awaken
in a new place,
but the hedgehog
chooses
to stumble out of deep
sleep for a new nest.
Too young,
Ava's choice
was made for her,
because she giggles
like the splinter of light
forcing itself through the seam
at her coffin's latch,
the way her warm breath
forced its way
through snow-covered
knitted mittens
months ago.
When she awakens—
alive,
yet still wearing
a death shroud—
she will smell
of pine
rather than her
mother's hands.

Avraham's Thunderstorm

Sobibor, 1943

Miles from here, lawn
mowers cut what stands

too tall—scissors to yards
of dandelions with faces

resembling children's drawings
of suns—petals spreading

like yellow flames over soot.
Miles from here, someone

milks a cow—offspring
long devoured—churns

milk to butter for sautéing
mushrooms and onions.

Miles from here, someone hunts
a squirrel with a .22 rifle

for stew sopped up
with dry bread. Miles from here,

a man embraces a tree,
climbs to the top. With a saw,

he cuts off each limb,
one by one.

He is confident in his control
over where it all falls, but strength

remains in the scent of sawdust
from a healthy tree. It hangs

in the air for days, weeks—
long after he has thrown

chopped wood into a stove's firebox.
People say they fear cemeteries,

because the ground never lets go
of the bodies it holds, but it

exhales steam, small flames of ruin.
People say they smell a storm

coming, feel it in their knees
and elbows. Up to a mile from here,

we sting their noses, ache
their bones.

Franz Stangl Orders the Construction of a "Zoo" for Trapped Foxes and Two Peacocks

Treblinka, 1943

CAGE 1: Franz Stangl's Vixen

Her eyes glowed red on the edge
of the forest. Most good people
fear the vixen's skulk, diseases,
bite, but when I opened my palm,
revealing a mound of crumbs,
she ate. It comforted me to give
her sustenance—to keep her alive.

Behind the chain link walls, I tame
her wildness while she screams
human in the night. I once reached
out to pet soft red fur, but she bared
white sharp teeth, ready to reveal red
under my skin. In that moment,
I saw myself in her.

CAGE 2: Sara's Cage

Our eyes dart in light
after the blindness inside trains.
No one laughs in a cage.
No one embraces the dark in a cage.
Cages do not properly contain our
wildness—it burns inside us. Behind
that door, chitter turns to silence,

wildness disappears into mist. Sometimes
littler ones hide under falling, dead—still
able to breathe through and after the gas.
Any living being will fight for one
more breath, hide for it if necessary.

I once saw *them* playing with *our*
children awaiting gas, awaiting
freedom from this place. In that moment,
I wished to be a child again,
to be deceived again.

Avraham on Freedom

Sobibor Uprising

Icarus's father, Daedalus, constructed wings out of peacock feathers and melted yahrzeit candles from all their ancestors. He was tired of the dead weighing him down—their memory in his name. He said to Icarus, *With these wings, we can fly over the labyrinth that traps us*. But when Icarus first tried on the wings, adjusting them on his shoulders, their weight left an impression in his skin like a string tied tight around a turtle's shell. He stood still for quite some time, staring over the edge of the cliff at the labyrinth's perimeter, waiting on wind to lift him. And then it happened—his father's push or a gust took him (he didn't care which). For once, nothing was in his way, nothing seemed like it could drag him down. The sun's warmth calmed him like his mother's breath, but too much of anything can be a bad thing. And just like that, as all his ancestors called his name through the heat, he knew he would never really leave the labyrinth. Wings a myth, but those yahrzeit candles real, and he realized in that moment, the only possibility of freedom was jumping off the cliff.

Sara's Uprising

Treblinka Uprising, August 2, 1943

The maggot
desires my flesh
so much, he leaves
his rifle out of reach.
I want out so much,
I draw a bomb
with my finger on his skin,
connecting his moles
like a constellation.
As I harden him, he
shoves me into the corner,
pants half-down. Larvae
sticky skin. Hot breath—
so much steam I could
draw a revolver
on a window. I never
look into their eyes,
but today,
I explore his—
dark clouds hovering
in the middle of it all
ready to spread.
Fireworks become
my freedom as one of our
men sneaks in, grabs the rifle
by the door, starts
our war.

Sara on the Train Ride to the Bergen-Belsen Displaced Persons Camp

July 1945

Mama stopped wearing her wristwatch
after I was born, but Papa never stopped
looking at his. Every evening, golden hands
slowed, seemingly aware and waiting for him
to wind them back to life the next morning.
Are windup soldiers and trains left in my dusty
toybox waiting on me to turn their keys?
Or did a German boy watch soldiers beat
drums, watch the unmoving clown conductor
smile ahead while wheels on the red and black
painted train spun forward? Or did he take
them apart to figure out the gears? Maybe
he threw them away—the weight of all
the rubble crushed them. The paint scratched
off so much that even if I returned and dug
them up, they would be unrecognizable.

Sara's Wedding Day

Bergen-Belsen Displaced Persons Camp, 1946

From under rubble,
you emerged—my
doorway, window—

gem
amongst rocks
for tombstones.

I—covered in moon
stone linen
rather than lace

(dead women never wear lace)—
stand under this chuppah
lit with your fire.

Clear glass breaks—
like early frost
after a stifling summer.

We rise together—
two flames from Shabbos
candles.

Henryk Błaszczyk's Cherries

Kielce, Poland Pogrom, July 4, 1946

I cannot tell you how many pie-sweet cherries covered the grass—blanket blood-spotted. I can tell you, I wanted them and grabbed them like a cat pawing a nest for red-speckled thrush eggs. I can tell you that after plucking them—stuffing my pillowcase brick-heavy—I stained my hands, mouth with red juice. I thought no one would care, but when I returned with a full belly, pillowcase empty—the way their survivors returned with change of clothes filling a pillowcase, bellies empty—Dad grabbed my shoulder, plum-bruised it, and asked, *Who plucked you?* Because I pointed to a tree of life, everyone else pointed limbs, making all their nests blood-speckled.

Sara on the Missing Children

Our missing children
are not taking pictures
with grandparents, clowns,
or storybook characters
at festivals or carnivals.
They never stood in lines
for hours to ride roller coasters
to only puke up candy
and ice cream. They never
stayed up late to watch fireworks.
They are not in treehouses
made with their daddies,
throwing pinecones as grenades
at squirrels. They are not
dancing like flames from fires
built from flint and steel
with chaperones. No one ever
gave them marshmallows
to roast on sticks and devour
in fabric foldout chairs
or canvas tents. They are not
hiding under twin beds
from monsters in closets.
They are not listening
for the crackling of footsteps
on leaves as friends finish
counting to twenty
behind trees, because they
became *it* in a game of tag
that no one warned them of
years ago.

Sara on Motherhood

August 1955

After seventeen years, a cicada
digs himself out of his egg grave.
As dirt held him all those years,
the way my body held my children,
did he desire freedom from his larva
shell the way the dead eventually
become free from pine coffins?
Did he desire the sensation of wind
holding up his wings and pushing him
along, the way it holds and pushes
ashes dropped from an urn?
Now, he and hundreds awaken
for nights of living, once nearly dead,
shedding their baby shells to mate. When
my toddler son holds up his trophy—
the cicada shell he pulled from the edge
of his wooden sandbox, saying,
Friend, I know that feeling of wanting
something hollow to come alive. When
my son plays with the shell until
it crumbles, crying, saying, *My friend*
broke, I know that feeling of destroying
something by loving it too much—
a wrinkled, torn photo taped together,
a memory too idyllic to be real.

Sara's Garden

May 1957

Uncombed strands—knotting
themselves together like clumps
of dried mud on my daughter's knees,
under her nails after planting
carrot and basil seeds—tap
on her shoulder, heat her
forehead and neck sweat
soaked. A shrub flowers to life—
she shrugs darkness away, brown
yarn whispering to her
brother as he draws a garden
made of red ovals for blossoms
and squiggly green lines for stems.
Beside them, blue scissor handle eyes
stare him down from the edge
of his art supply box. He
bouquets her threads in his hand
the way she grabs at the shrub's
blonde flowers, pruned petals
escaping violence
as the grass catches them.

Sara's Faith

after the painting, "Camp Synagogue, Saint Cyprien, 1941", by Felix Nussbaum

Like the man pausing,
        not entering shul,
I struggle with whether
to enter or deny my Judaism.

I struggle with whether
the prayer shawl is a baby blanket—
a puerile crutch
        always offering comfort—
or a thick hand sewn quilt
only useful during winter storms.

While traveling abroad to nations
        burying traces
of barbed wire, leaving a single bone
        without the body,
a single shoe without a mate,
I became accustomed
        to hiding my star
necklace under my shirt
the way ravens cache food
under leaves
when competing
        for rations.

Do I neglect the powder train
of men praying
        in a shack
rather than an elaborate synagogue?
Or do I defy ruin
by wearing my gold star,
the way Hasidic men
        wear prayer shawls,
while entering the synagogue—
whether a shack, rows of benches

in a field by a lake, or a mosaic
and stained glass decorated building
with centuries-old Torahs—
while my belief in
            G-d is fleeting
like a conspiracy of ravens flying
toward or away from shul?

Franz Stangl's Letter to His Wife from Düsseldorf Prison

Dear Therese,

I apologize for being their windvane—pointing east or slashing air with a riding crop as they came off trains. Sometimes I swung it in my hand to watch them unhinge. Guards here swing batons like that.

I apologize for wearing white—a dove amongst pigeons. These guards—ravens—thrive off decay. Here, cornflowers rot slowly in vases, but I preferred speed of herbicide.

I apologize for adrenaline, sun, wind. I enjoyed suitcases full of cookies and jars of marmalade. I also enjoyed the numbing of senses. I never liked the smell of compost. I never liked touching rose petals. I held on tight to stems, avoided thorns, and kept petals fresh.

Overtime, whiteness loses its richness; skin loses its elasticity. Without nourishment, the surface erodes, reveals what it covers. Now that everyone sees my filthy hands, this cage gets smaller every day, and bars obstruct faces on the other side. I apologize for having been there and being here.

Yours,

Franz
27. June 1971

Sara Learns of Franz Stangl's Death

June 28, 1971

I rub my hands together—crumble
clumps of bath salts, lather
soap on skin as bubbles multiply
like blisters from chemical burns.
Too much scrubbing will redden
what holds us together or make it
crack like stale bread. The past might
always remain under fingernails,
in wrinkles as memory whirlpools
down a drain, murmurs until
it disappears. Steam rises—vanishes
hot clouds—forgetting that as water
it once cooled, soothed. Any river
can become a mikveh, smoothing
sharp edges off rocks over time,
the way rain erases names off
tombstones. Faraway, a mountain
reshapes itself in a flood, buries
veils, photos, all that lies at its base.
Here, joy fills an arroyo after a drought
as I listen to someone else's laughter—
a child's void of chains, but we link
arms together in dance. I touch
my fingers to a piano, and it all
comes back to me—Mama and I
in a duet at the piano playing, singing
at Passover—*Then came the Holy One*
who slew the Angel of Death. I grab
at delight like a faint star.
When I finally catch it, I will
never let go of that light
no matter how dim it appears.

Historical Notes

"Esther's Curfew":
On March 29, 1516, by a degree of the chief magistrate of Venice, a walled and gated ghetto was established to segregate Jews from the rest of the population. Jews were taxed higher for living in the ghetto, and Christians had to move out when the ghetto was officially established. However, Jews were allowed to exit freely for a few hours each day, which allowed Christians to do business with Jews and walk through the ghetto to other parts of the city. When Napoleon took control of Venice in 1797, the gates were removed.

"Rivka Survives":
On June 23, 1919, during the Ukraine Civil War, belligerents raped thirty-five Jewish women and murdered forty-five Jews.

"Sara Visits Avraham's Tailor Shop":
The inspiration for the name "Sara" came from the Executive Order on the Law on the Alteration of Family and Personal Names, which was signed on August 17, 1938. The law required German Jews with "non-Jewish" first names to add "Sara" or "Israel" (respectively, depending on their gender) as their middle names on their passports and identity cards to signify their separation from the rest of the German population.

"Consul General Feng-Shan Ho and Rabbi Shimon Sholom Kalish Discuss the Jewish Question":
Feng-Shan Ho was the Chinese Consul General in Vienna from 1938 until 1940 and saved thousands of Jews by issuing visas for safe travel to Shanghai.

"Avraham's Tailor Shop":
Kristallnacht (Night of Broken Glass) refers to a wave of pogroms that occurred throughout Nazi Germany and occupied territories. During these pogroms, Nazis destroyed Jewish homes, businesses, and synagogues. Additionally, they murdered at least one hundred Jews.

"Chaja Kubrzanska's Bath":
On June 23, 1941, Germans took control of Jedwabne, Poland. On June 25, 1941, non-Jewish Polish men started a pogrom in Jedwabne. A local priest convinced the mob to stop by telling them that Germans would take care of the situation. However, on July 10, 1941, with Nazi encouragement, non-Jewish Poles murdered their Jewish neighbors using various weapons and by burning them alive in a barn.

"Matya's Separation":
On June 28, 1941, non-Jewish Poles in Szczuczyn, Poland murdered about 300 of their wealthy Jewish neighbors with axes.

"Shmuel's Loss":
On July 4 and 5, 1941, Polish men wielding axes and clubs murdered dozens of their Jewish neighbors in Wąsosz and then looted their homes.

"Franz Stangl's White Clothes":
Franz Stangl was the commandant of Sobibor from April 1942 until August 1942 and was also the commandant of Treblinka from September 1, 1942 until August 1943. Under his command, Nazis murdered hundreds of thousands of Jews.

"Mikhail's Soup":
On November 7 and 20, 1941, Nazis murdered thousands of Jews from the Minsk Ghetto. Beginning November 11, trains filled with German Jews arrived to fill the homes of the dead.

"Sara's Bed":
עצי חיים (pronounced Atzei Chaim) are Torah rollers. The words mean "trees of life" in Hebrew.

"The Infanticide of Puah":
According to Stanisława Leszczyńska, a survivor (and midwife as prisoner) of Auschwitz, at least 3,000 babies were born in Auschwitz. However, "Sister Klara," a German midwife who was sent there for infanticide, drowned many of them immediately after birth in a bucket of water. Sometimes the children born with blue eyes were sent to Germany for adoption.

"Irena Sendler Saves Ava":
Irena Sendler was the director of the Department for the Care of Jewish Children for the underground Council for Aid to Jews (the Polish code name for the organization was Zegota). Under her leadership, thousands of Jewish children were rescued by being smuggled out of ghettos into orphanages, convents, and foster homes.

"Avraham on Freedom":
On October 14, 1943, Jewish prisoners of Sobibor revolted, killing eleven Nazis with axes while roughly 300 prisoners escaped.

"Sara's Uprising":
On August 2, 1943, Jewish prisoners of Treblinka revolted. Even though many resistance fighters died during the uprising, it was successful due to Franz Stangl's reassignment and the entire camp closing shortly afterwards. Archival research conducted by fellows at Yad Vashem revealed that women in camp brothels were integral to the success of camp uprisings.

"Henryk Błaszczyk's Cherries":
On July 4, 1946, Polish soldiers, police officers, and civilians murdered forty-two Jews in Kielce, Poland, because they believed that Jewish refugees returning from concentration camps kidnapped a non-Jewish Polish boy, Henryk Błaszczyk.

"Sara on the Train Ride to the Bergen-Belsen Displaced Persons Camp":
At the end of World War II, survivors of concentration camps had nowhere to go, because their former homes and communities had been destroyed. Displaced person (DP) camps were established to hold these refugees from 1945 until 1951. The former Bergen-Belsen concentration camp was transformed into the largest DP camp in Europe. According to data from Yad Vashem, DP camps had the highest birth rates in the world at that time.

"Sara Learns of Franz Stangl's Death":
Franz Stangl died in Düsseldorf Prison of a heart attack on June 28, 1971.

About the Author

Liz Marlow earned her MBA from the University of Memphis, MFA from Western Michigan University, and undergraduate degree from the University of Tennessee at Chattanooga. She is the founding and current editor of *Minyan Magazine.* She has formerly served as Coeditor and Managing Editor of Slapering Hol Press. She was also a reader for New Issues Press and Orange Blossom Review. Her work has appeared in dozens of journals and anthologies, including *Best Small Fictions, The Idaho Review, the minnesota review, Nimrod International Journal,* and *Valparaiso Poetry Review.* She has received Pushcart, Best New Poets, Best Small Fictions, Best Microfiction, and Best of the Net nominations. She is the 2019 recipient of the Slapering Hol Press Chapbook Competition.

Her debut full-length poetry collection, *The Ground Never Lets Go* (Moon Tide Press, 2026), was previously a finalist for the Blue Light Book Award from Blue Light Press in 2025, the Word Works' Washington Prize in 2023, Gerald Cable Book Award from Silverfish Review Press in 2023, Longleaf Press Book Contest in 2022, Wheelbarrow Books Poetry Prize in 2022, and Colorado Prize for Poetry in 2021 and 2022. It was also a semifinalist for the St. Lawrence Book Award from Black Lawrence Press in 2023 and the Lexi Rudinsky First

Book Prize from Persea Books in 2022. Additionally, her chapbook, *They Become Stars* (Slapering Hol Press, 2020) was a finalist for the Tomaž Šalamun Prize in 2019 and winner of the Slapering Hol Press Chapbook Competition in 2019.

Acknowledgements

Special thanks to the editors of the publications in which poems from *The Ground Never Lets Go* first appeared, often in an altered version and/or with a different title.

Atticus Review
G-d
Avraham's Tailor Shop
Sara's Letter to Her Grandparents, Berlin
Sara's Migration
Mikhail's Letter, Minsk Ghetto

Beloit Poetry Journal
Sara on the Train Ride to the Bergen-Belsen Displaced Persons Camp

Gyroscope Review
Sara's First Lesson with Her New Piano Teacher

Harbor Review
Rabbi Avigdor Białostocki's Dance

The Heartland Review
Sara's Garden

The Idaho Review
Henryk Błaszczyk's Cherries

The Inflectionist Review
Franz Stangl's White Clothes
Sara Contemplates Where Her Parents Might Be
Sara Learns of Franz Stangl's Death

Jet Fuel Review
Rivka Survives
Sara and the Fox

The MacGuffin
Franz Stangl Orders the Construction of a "Zoo" for Trapped Foxes and Two Peacocks
Sara's Uprising

Mud Season Review—The Take
Chaja Kubrzanska's Bath

The Night Heron Barks
Sara Visits Avraham's Tailor Shop
Sara Spins Her Dreidel the Night Before Her Father, Avraham, Leaves to Find Work
Avraham and the Fence

Nimrod International Journal
Avraham Recalls His Last Rosh Hashanah as a Married Man
Avraham's Thunderstorm

Open: Journal of Arts & Letters
Mikhail's Soup
Avraham's New Home
Sara's Faith

Orange Blossom Review
Irena Sendler Smuggles Ava Out of the Ghetto

Ran Off with the Star Bassoon
Franz Stangl's Letter to His Wife from Düsseldorf Prison

The Rumpus—Enough
Sara on the Missing Children

Split Rock Review
Franz Stangl's Treblinka

Small Orange
Sara's Uniform

Stoneboat Literary Journal
Sara on Motherhood

Stonecoast Review
Sara's Mother Teaches Her How to Prepare Onion Soup
Sara Imagines Herself a Golem
Sara's Hunger

Superstition Review
Avraham's Freedom

The Tusculum Review
Avraham Leaves His Family Behind to Find Work

Vestal Review
The Infanticide of Puah

Wilderness House Literary Review
German Jews Travel from Genoa, Italy to Shanghai via the SS Victoria Cruise Liner

Yemassee
Esther's Curfew

Special thanks to the editors of *Objects in This Mirror: An Anthology of Legacy* (Press 53, 2025) for republishing "Sara's Uniform" and "Avraham on Freedom."

"Consul General Feng-Shan Ho and Rabbi Shimon Sholom Kalish Discuss the Jewish Question" was included in the chapbook, *They Become Stars*, which was the winner of the 2019 Slapering Hol Press Chapbook Competition.

Special thanks to the editors of *Jet Fuel Review* for nominating "Rivka Survives" for a Pushcart Prize and for inclusion in *The Best Small Fictions.*

"Rivka Survives" was in *The Best Small Fictions 2022* (Sonder Press, 2022).

Special thanks to the editors of *The Inflectionist Review* for nominating "Sara Learns of Franz Stangl's Death" for a Pushcart Prize.

Special thanks to the editors of *The Night Heron Barks* for nominating "Sara Visits Avraham's Tailor Shop" for a Pushcart Prize and inclusion in *Best New Poets.* Additional thanks for nominating "Sara Spins Her Dreidel the Night Before Her Father, Avraham, Leaves to Find Work" for inclusion in the *Best of the Net* anthology.

Special thanks to the editors of *The MacGuffin* for nominating "Franz Stangl Orders the Construction of a 'Zoo' for Trapped Foxes and Two Peacocks" for inclusion in *Best New Poets.*

Special thanks to the editors of *Vestal Review* for nominating "The Infanticide of Puah" for inclusion in the *Best Microfiction* anthology.

"Avraham's Last Rosh Hashanah" was a finalist in *New South's* 2021 Annual Writing Contest and a semifinalist for *Nimrod International Journal's* 2021 Pablo Neruda Prize for Poetry.

"Avraham's Thunderstorm" was also a semifinalist for *Nimrod International Journal's* 2021 Pablo Neruda Prize for Poetry.

Henryk Błaszczyk's Cherries" and "Sara's Hunger" (originally titled "Lilith's Hunger") were longlisted for *Poetry International's* 2020 C.P. Cavafy Prize.

Also Available from Moon Tide Press

Afterburn, Rebecca Evans (2026)
Not So Fast, Sarah McMahon (2026)
The Elephant of Surprise, Charles Harper Webb (2026)
Outliving Michael, Steven Reigns (2025)
Prayers With a Side of Cash, Kathleen Florence (2025)
Somewhere, a Playground, Rich Ferguson (2025)
The Tautology of Water, Giovanni Boskovich (2025)
Take Care, Mark Danowsky (2025)
Dilapitatia, Kelly Gray (2025)
Reluctant Prophets, J.D. Isip (2025)
Enormous Blue Umbrella, Donna Hilbert (2025)
Sky Leaning Toward Winter, Terri Niccum (2024)
Living the Sundown: A Caregiving Memoir, G. Murray Thomas (2024)
Figure Study, Kathryn de Lancellotti (2024)
Suffer for This: Love, Sex, Marriage, & Rock 'N' Roll, Victor D. Infante (2024)
What Blooms in the Dark, Emily J. Mundy (2024)
Fable, Bryn Wickerd (2024)
Diamond Bars 2, David A. Romero (2024)
Safe Handling, Rebecca Evans (2024)
More Jerkumstances: New & Selected Poems, Barbara Eknoian (2024)
Dissection Day, Ally McGregor (2023)
He's a Color Until He's Not, Christian Hanz Lozada (2023)
The Language of Fractions, Nicelle Davis (2023)
Paradise Anonymous, Oriana Ivy (2023)
Now You Are a Missing Person, Susan Hayden (2023)
Maze Mouth, Brian Sonia-Wallace (2023)
Tangled by Blood, Rebecca Evans (2023)
Another Way of Loving Death, Jeremy Ra (2023)
Kissing the Wound, J.D. Isip (2023)
Feed It to the River, Terhi K. Cherry (2022)
Beat Not Beat: An Anthology of California Poets Screwing on the Beat and Post-Beat Tradition (2022)
When There Are Nine: Poems Celebrating the Life and Achievements of Ruth Bader Ginsburg (2022)
The Knife Thrower's Daughter, Terri Niccum (2022)

2 Revere Place, Aruni Wijesinghe (2022)
Here Go the Knives, Kelsey Bryan-Zwick (2022)
Trumpets in the Sky, Jerry Garcia (2022)
Threnody, Donna Hilbert (2022)
A Burning Lake of Paper Suns, Ellen Webre (2021)
Instructions for an Animal Body, Kelly Gray (2021)
*Head *V* Heart: New & Selected Poems*, Rob Sturma (2021)
*Sh!t Men Say to Me: A Poetry Anthology in Response t
o Toxic Masculinity* (2021)
Flower Grand First, Gustavo Hernandez (2021)
Everything is Radiant Between the Hates, Rich Ferguson (2020)
When the Pain Starts: Poetry as Sequential Art,
Alan Passman (2020)
This Place Could Be Haunted If I Didn't Believe in Love,
Lincoln McElwee (2020)
Impossible Thirst, Kathryn de Lancellotti (2020)
Lullabies for End Times, Jennifer Bradpiece (2020)
Crabgrass World, Robin Axworthy (2020)
Contortionist Tongue, Dania Ayah Alkhouli (2020)
The only thing that makes sense is to grow, Scott Ferry (2020)
Dead Letter Box, Terri Niccum (2019)
Tea and Subtitles: Selected Poems 1999-2019, Michael Miller (2019)
At the Table of the Unknown, Alexandra Umlas (2019)
The Book of Rabbits, Vince Trimboli (2019)
Everything I Write Is a Love Song to the World,
David McIntire (2019)
Letters to the Leader, HanaLena Fennel (2019)
Darwin's Garden, Lee Rossi (2019)
Dark Ink: A Poetry Anthology Inspired by Horror (2018)
Drop and Dazzle, Peggy Dobreer (2018)
Junkie Wife, Alexis Rhone Fancher (2018)
The Moon, My Lover, My Mother, & the Dog, Daniel McGinn (2018)
Lullaby of Teeth: An Anthology of Southern California Poetry (2017)
Angels in Seven, Michael Miller (2016)
A Likely Story, Robbi Nester (2014)
Embers on the Stairs, Ruth Bavetta (2014)
The Green of Sunset, John Brantingham (2013)
The Savagery of Bone, Timothy Matthew Perez (2013)
The Silence of Doorways, Sharon Venezio (2013)

Cosmos: An Anthology of Southern California Poetry (2012)
Straws and Shadows, Irena Praitis (2012)
In the Lake of Your Bones, Peggy Dobreer (2012)
I Was Building Up to Something, Susan Davis (2011)
Hopeless Cases, Michael Kramer (2011)
One World, Gail Newman (2011)
What We Ache For, Eric Morago (2010)
Now and Then, Lee Mallory (2009)
Pop Art: An Anthology of Southern California Poetry (2009)
In the Heaven of Never Before, Carine Topal (2008)
A Wild Region, Kate Buckley (2008)
Carving in Bone: An Anthology of Orange County Poetry (2007)
Kindness from a Dark God, Ben Trigg (2007)
A Thin Strand of Lights, Ricki Mandeville (2006)
Sleepyhead Assassins, Mindy Nettifee (2006)
Tide Pools: An Anthology of Orange County Poetry (2006)
Lost American Nights: Lyrics & Poems, Michael Ubaldini (2006)

Patrons

Moon Tide Press would like to thank the following people for their support in helping publish the finest poetry from the Southern California region. To sign up as a patron, visit www.moontidepress.com or send an email to publisher@moontidepress.com.

Anonymous
Robin Axworthy
Conner Brenner
Nicole Connolly
Bill Cushing
Susan Davis
Kristen Baum DeBeasi
Peggy Dobreer
Kate Gale
Dennis Gowans
Alexis Rhone Fancher
HanaLena Fennel
Half Off Books & Brad T. Cox
Donna Hilbert
Jim & Vicky Hoggatt
Michael Kramer
Ron Koertge & Bianca Richards
Gary Jacobelly
Ray & Christi Lacoste
Jeffery Lewis
Zachary & Tammy Locklin
Lincoln McElwee
David McIntire
José Enrique Medina
Michael Miller &
Rachanee Srisavasdi
Michelle & Robert Miller
Ronny & Richard Morago
Terri Niccum
Andrew November
Jeremy Ra
Luke & Mia Salazar
Jennifer Smith
Roger Sponder
Andrew Turner
Rex Wilder
Mariano Zaro
Wes Bryan Zwick

www.ingramcontent.com/pod-product-compliance
Lightning Source LLC
LaVergne TN
LVHW051018080826
845145LV00009B/2681

* 9 7 8 1 9 5 7 7 9 9 9 9 5 *